THE WEAPONS ENCYCLOPÆDIA
TANK AIRCRAFT AFV SHIP ARTILLERY VEHICLES SECRET WEAPON

TWE-023 ENG

FIAT 3000 & FIAT 2000

THE WEAPONS ENCYCLOPAEDIA

EDITORIAL STAFF
Luca Cristini, Paolo Crippa.

ACADEMIC STAFF
Enrico Acerbi, Massimiliano Afiero, Aldo Antonicelli, Ruggero Calò, Luigi Carretta, Flavio Chistè, Anna Cristini, Carlo Cucut, Salvo Fagone, Enrico Finazzer, Arturo Giusti, Björn Huber, Andrea Lombardi, Aymeric Lopez, Marco Lucchetti, Gabriele Malavoglia, Luigi Manes, Giovanni Maressi, Francesco Mattesini, Daniele Notaro, Péter Mujzer, Federico Peirani, Alberto Peruffo, Maurizio Raggi, Andrea Alberto Tallillo, Antonio Tallillo, Massimo Zorza.

PUBLISHED BY
Luca Cristini Editore (Soldiershop), via Orio, 35/4 - 24050 Zanica (BG) ITALY.

DISTRIBUTION BY
Soldiershop - www.soldiershop.com, Amazon, Ingram Spark, Berliner Zinnfigurem (D), LaFeltrinelli, Mondadori, Libera Editorial (Spain), Google book (eBook), Kobo, (eBoook), Apple Book (eBook).

PUBLISHING'S NOTES
None of unpublished images or text of our book may be reproduced in any format without the expressed written permission of Luca Cristini Editore (already Soldiershop.com) when not indicate as marked with license creative commons 3.0 or 4.0. Luca Cristini Editore has made every reasonable effort to locate, contact and acknowledge rights holders and to correctly apply terms and conditions to Content. Every effort has been made to trace the copyright of all the photographs. If there are unintentional omissions, please contact the publisher in writing at: info@soldiershop.com, who will correct all subsequent editions.

LICENSES COMMONS
This book may utilize part of material marked with license creative commons 3.0 or 4.0 (CC BY 4.0), (CC BY-ND 4.0), (CC BY-SA 4.0) or (CC0 1.0). We give appropriate attribution credit and indicate if change were made in the acknowledgments field. Our WTW books series utilize only fonts licensed under the SIL Open Font License or other free use license.

CONTRIBUTORS OF THIS VOLUME & ACKNOWLEDGEMENTS
Ringraziamo i principali collaboratori di questo numero: I profili dei carri sono tutti dell'autore. Le colorazioni delle foto sono di Anna Cristini. Ringraziamenti particolari a istituzioni nazionali e/o private quali: Stato Maggiore dell'esercito, Archivio di Stato, Bundesarchiv, Nara, Library of Congress, Wikipedia, USAF, Signal magazine, Cronache di guerra, Fronte di guerra, IWM, Australian War Museum, ecc. A P.Crippa, A.Lopez, Péter Mujzer, L.Manes, C.Cucut, archivi Tallillo. Model Victoria (www.modelvictoria.it) ecc. per avere messo a disposizione immagini o altro dei loro archivi.

For a complete list of Soldiershop titles, or for every information please contact us on our website: www.soldiershop.com or www.cristinieditore.com. E-mail: info@soldiershop.com. Keep up to date on Facebook https://www.facebook.com/soldiershop.publishing

Title: **FIAT 3000 & FIAT 2000** Code.: **TWE-023 EN**
Series by L. S. Cristini
ISBN code: 9791255891147 First edition May 2024
THE WEAPONS ENCYCLOPAEDIA (SOLDIERSHOP) is a trademark of Luca Cristini Editore

THE WEAPONS ENCYCLOPÆDIA
TANK AIRCRAFT AFV SHIP ARTILLERY VEHICLES SECRET WEAPON

FIAT 3000
& FIAT 2000

LUCA STEFANO CRISTINI

BOOK SERIES FOR MODELERS & COLLECTORS

CONTENTS

FIAT 2000 .... pag. 5
- Development .... pag. 5
- Technical features .... pag. 5
- Operational use .... pag. 6

FIAT 3000 .... pag. 13
- Development .... pag. 13
- Technical features .... pag. 15
- Armament .... pag. 18

Le versioni dei mezzi .... pag. 23

Impiego operativo .... pag. 31

Mimetica e segni distintivi .... pag. 49

Produzione ed esportazione .... pag. 55

Scheda tecnica .... pag. 57

Bibliografia .... pag. 58

▲ Beautiful photo of a FIAT 2000 No.2 taken in May 1930, with all eight crew members posing on the tank. Source unknown. Author's colouring.

FIAT 2000

Let's jump back and talk about the FIAT 3000's predecessor first. Although it is true that Italy began exploring the armoured car sector almost immediately, the first real Italian tank project was only initiated in 1916, mainly by a certain captain named Luigi Cassali. His vision was to create an armoured car capable of moving through the terrain, equipped with two turrets fitted with machine guns. This vehicle was actually built by the Pavesi company, experts in off-road vehicles. However, the project, known as the FIAT 1000, was abandoned after tests revealed limitations in its engineering.

DEVELOPMENT

Then, in August 1916, a new project, the FIAT 2000, began. Its actual construction began about two months later, in October of the same year. This project had to be realised as quickly as possible, so it was initially started semi-privately before the Army had even established the requirements; the engineers in charge were the pragmatic Carlo Cavalli and the imaginative Giulio Cesare Cappa. The first prototype was completed in June 1917, hence the alternative name 'Type 17'. The **FIAT 2000 Mod. 17** was a heavy (very heavy) tank and only two examples were produced, one in 1917 and one in 1918. Because of its armour, the thickest among the coeval tanks, at 40 tonnes it was the heaviest tank produced during the First World War, with the exception of the never-completed German 120-tonne K-Wagen. Besides its weight, it was distinguished by some innovative solutions, such as the fully rotating turret (also present on the French Renault FT tank) armed with a cannon and the engine compartment separated from the crew compartment. Initially, the prototype lacked machine gun mounts and featured a cylindrical turret with a flat roof. However, this turret was soon replaced by a domed construction. The design of the FIAT 2000 was extraordinarily advanced for its time, as it was the first operational tank to be equipped with a turret, a solution that proved to be fundamental for the evolution of armoured vehicles.

TECHNICAL FEATURES

The hull of the FIAT 2000 Mod. 17 was composed of a strong casemate of slightly inclined bolted armour, 20 millimetres thick on the sides and 15 millimetres thick on the top and bottom of the hull. The interior of the vehicle was divided into two separate compartments: the lower engine compartment housed the engine, transmission, clutches and other mechanical components, while the combat cockpit above was accessible through an armoured hatch on the right side.
The main armament consisted of a specially adapted 65/17 Mod. 1908/1913 companion gun mounted in a hemispherical turret consisting of four sheet metal segments and a dome with a lifting hook. The turret had a vertical slit for the cannon and a semi-circular shield integral with the shaft, as well as an opening for the aiming system on the left side. The turret was fully rotatable through 360° and allowed a wide elevation firing range, from -10° to +75°, allowing the piece to be used for curved firing as well.
The secondary armament comprised seven water-cooled FIAT-Revelli Mod. 1914 6.5 mm machine guns, positioned on mounts with semi-circular shields that adapted to the casemate at various swing angles. The machine guns were arranged at the corners of the casemate, on the sides and at the rear, ensuring simultaneous coverage on all firing sectors.
The crew, consisting of 10 soldiers, filled the fighting compartment. The casemate had an armoured cabin for the driver at the front, with a large opening at the front equipped with an armoured door and closable loopholes at the sides. The seven gunners had gun openings and loopholes with flaps on the sides and rear. The gunner and assistant gunner occupied the turret.
The petrol engine, a 21,200 cm^3 FIAT A12 with 6 in-line vertical cylinders, was located at the rear of the engine compartment. With a power output of 250 hp at 1,400 rpm, the engine allowed the vehicle to reach a top speed of 7.5 km/h. The water-cooling system included a rear radiator protected by a grille. Despite a 600-litre fuel tank, the range was limited to 75 km. The engine transmitted motion through a 4-speed and 2 reverse gears with a gearbox, controlled by the main clutch, to the two front drive wheels.

The rolling train, protected by armoured side skirts, allowed the vehicle to overcome obstacles such as trenches of up to 3.5 metres, steps of 1 metre and slopes of up to 40°, and to ford up to 1 metre of water. The tracks consisted of 45 cm wide ribbed steel plates, with leaf spring suspension on four oscillating carriages on each side, plus two fixed rollers at the ends.

OPERATIONAL USE

Despite the nickname *'the heaviest tank of the First World War'*, this is not entirely accurate, as the FIAT 2000 never actually saw combat during the First World War. The humble order of 50 tanks was never completed and only two prototypes were produced. After the war, the FIAT 2000 was displayed as one of the weapons used 'to defeat the enemy' and the two completed prototypes were sent to Libya to fight the guerrilla forces, along with other tanks purchased from France, in a special unit, the Autonomous Assault Tank Battery.

In Libya, the FIAT tank proved to be able to reach an average speed of 4 km/h and so, after two months, its career came to an end, as it was unable to keep up with the enemy's rapid movements. One remained in Tripoli and the other was sent to Italy in the spring of 1919, where it performed before the King at the Stadium in Rome. The tank performed convincingly: it climbed a 1.1 m wall, then faced another 3.5 m wall, which it knocked down with its weight. It then successfully crossed a 3 m wide trench and felled several trees. Despite this impressive performance, it failed to revive interest in the heavy tank and was thus abandoned. The FIAT 2000 that survived in Rome was left in a depot for several years, until it was sent by order of Colonel Maltese to Fort Tiburtino, almost catching fire during transport. In 1934 it was seen again in a parade at Campo Dux, after being repainted and rearmed, with two 37/40 mm cannons instead of the front machine guns. Later, it is said to have been turned into a monument in Bologna, after which its fate is unknown.

A curiosity: in March 2017, a committee made up of three associations joined forces with the aim of promoting the construction of a replica of the FIAT 2000 in exact scale and weight, making it functional. From June 2017 to October 2018, their efforts focused on the search for the technical documentation needed to completely redraw the vehicle's construction plan, supplementing the gaps in the original material preserved in Italy but still existing abroad. On 15 November 2018, with the conclusion of the design phase, the construction of the tank began in Montecchio Maggiore, overseen by the Associazione Nazionale Carristi d'Italia, the 'Cultori della Storia delle Forze Armate' Association and the 'Raggruppamento SPA' Cultural Association. The replica of the FIAT 2000 was completed in November 2020 and is now on display at the Carristi Memorial in the Museo delle Forze Armate 1914-1945 in Montecchio Maggiore.

▲ Prototype of the FIAT 2000 during tests in late 1917 and early 1918.

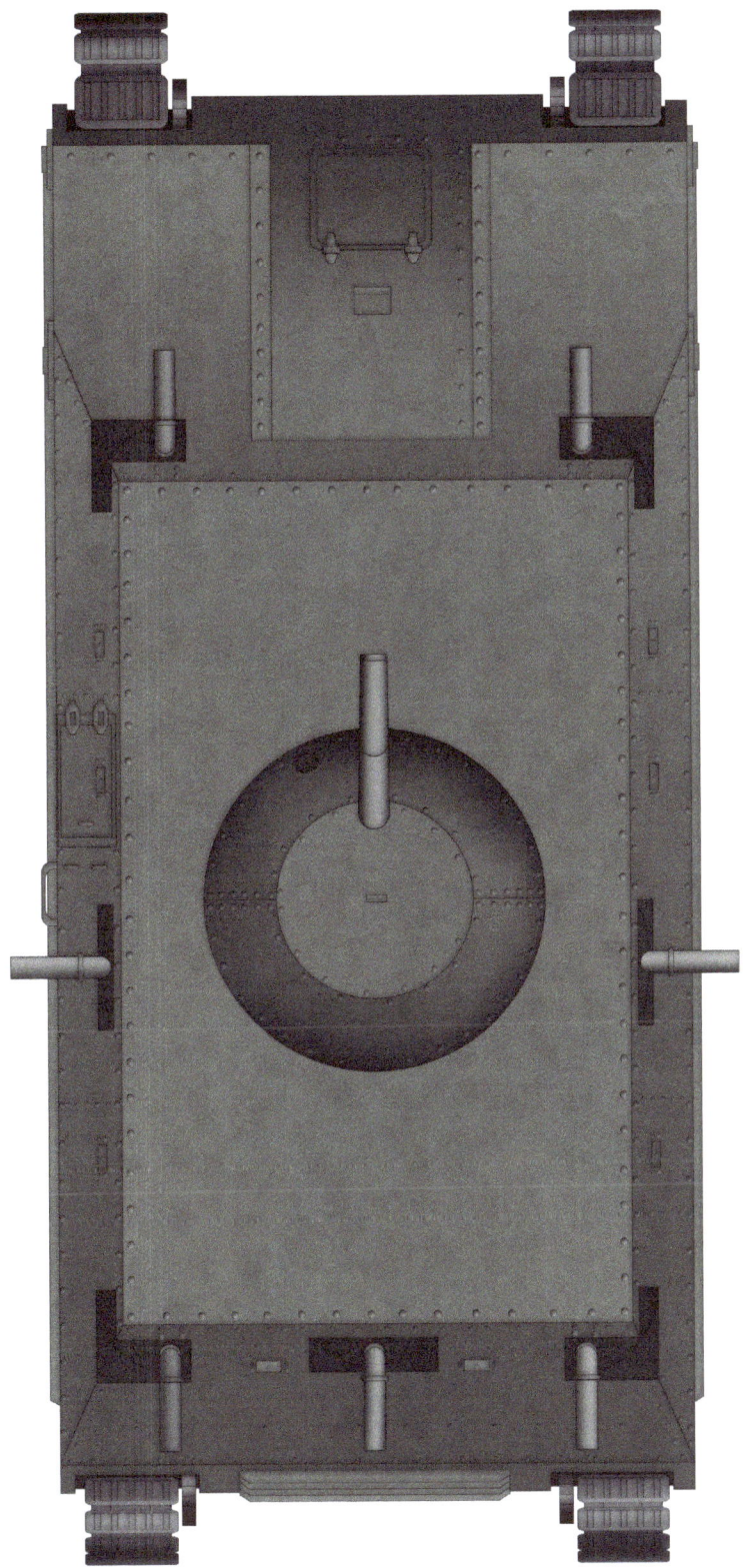

▲ FIAT 2000 profile seen from above

▲ FIAT 2000 profile front and rear view

FIAT 2000 GREY-GREEN VERSION, 1918 ITALY

FIAT 2000 CAMOUFLAGE VERSION, 1918 ITALY

▲ The giant FIAT 2000, symbolically 'escorted' by a balilla and a frontman.

◀ Italian officers next to FIAT 2000, mid-1918.

▼ This picture shows the tonnage of the FIAT 2000 next to smaller vehicles such as the Schneider CA-1, the Renault FT and the FIAT 3000 on the left.

ANSALDO-FIAT L5/21 (3000) LIGHT TANK (MODEL 1921), ITALY 1920-1930

▲ The FIAT 300 was derived directly from the French FT-17, and was therefore conceived towards the end of the Great War. The Model 21 was the first to be built in series.

FIAT 3000

The **FIAT 3000** was an important vehicle in the armament of the Italian army, entering service after the First World War. Produced in two versions, the Model 1921 and Model 1930, this light tank was essential for Italian armoured units until the 1930s. Originally based on the French Renault FT, it featured significant improvements such as a more powerful engine and an optimised interior layout. The FIAT 3000 represents an important chapter in the history of the Italian army, as it was one of the first tanks to be significantly deployed after the First World War, and allowed Italian crews to gain experience in the use of tanks, preparing them for future challenges on the battlefield.

DEVELOPMENT

Before the First World War, the Royal Italian Army was already distinguished by the use of armoured vehicles, as demonstrated by the use of the FIAT Arsenale armoured car during the Italian-Turkish War of 1911-1912. However, the development of its own armoured vehicles was initially slow, with only paper plans available in 1914, at the outbreak of the Great War.

FIAT started to develop a heavy tank, the FIAT 2000, but the process was slowed down by the lack of technical knowledge and the inexperience of Italian engineers in the field of armoured vehicles. The first prototype was only completed in 1917.

▲ FIAT 3000 model 1921 in the yard of the FIAT factory, ready for delivery. Web source. Author colouring.

▲ FIAT 3000 mod. 21 assault tank, first version. Image taken at Forte Tiburtino (Rome). This tank, as indicated by the white triangle in the turret, marks it as the command tank of the 2nd platoon.

Consequently, the Regio Esercito requested the help of Allied France and obtained four Renault FT tanks between 1917 and 1918, which were intensively tested. In addition to the Renault FTs, France provided a Schneider CA for training, but did not allow licensed production in Italy. In November 1918, the Regio Esercito decided to produce the tank under licence in Italy, entrusting the task to a consortium of Italian companies: Ansaldo, Armstrong Vickers, Breda, FIAT and Terni.

After the end of the war, an order for 1,400 Renault FTs to be produced under licence was cancelled. However, in 1919, 100 FIAT tanks were ordered, with modifications made to the original French design. The prototype was completed in 1920 and testing began in 1921. Finally, in 1923, the model was officially adopted as the FIAT 3000 Assault Tank, with further improvements made later, marking a turning point in the evolution of Italian tanks.

After the first crew training in 1923 in Belluno, northern Italy, the FIAT 3000 underwent further modifications. The production version, compared to the prototype, no longer featured the two front access doors inspired by the original Renault FT. Later, the vehicle was again improved, with lengthened tracks and improved wheels.

Between 1928 and 1929, a new model was developed, designated FIAT 3000 B, later renamed FIAT 3000 Model 1930. This new model was equipped with an upgraded engine and a cannon in the turret instead of two machine guns. The first tests of the vehicle took place during manoeuvres in Val Varaita, Piedmont, in 1929.

The vehicle changed name several times over the years, reflecting the evolution of Italian military thinking. After 1938, with Italy's entry into World War II, models armed with machine guns were renamed the Carro Armato Model 1921 and those with cannon the Carro Armato Model 1930.

During its operational life, the FIAT 3000 went through several designations, reflecting changing mili-

▲ FIAT 3000 mod.21 assault tank, first version.

tary strategies. From 1938, with Italy's entry into World War II, it was classified as a light tank, like all tanks under 7 tonnes. Thus, the FIAT 3000 crossed the three general classes of tanks from heavy to medium to light during its active service, a distinction probably unique in the history of armoured vehicles.

TECHNICAL FEATURES

The FIAT 3000 Mod.21 adopted a similar general configuration to its 'parent' the Renault FT-17, with tracks for propulsion and a 360° rotating turret, but differed externally in some distinctive features. The **turret**, larger than the French tank, was equipped exclusively with machine guns, while the tank underwent modifications and the rear of the hull was redesigned. These modifications, along with other upgrades, gave the FIAT 3000 greater effectiveness on the battlefield.

One of the key innovations was the lower centre of gravity, achieved through an optimised distribution of internal components and positioning of the engine. The **engine**, more powerful than the Renault FT with an output of 50 hp compared to the 40 hp of the French model, was mounted transversely, as opposed to the longitudinal arrangement of the FT. This choice not only helped reduce the overall weight of the vehicle, but also simplified the transmission and shortened the housing, thus improving agility and manoeuvrability.

The vanadium steel **armour** offered adequate protection against machine guns and shrapnel, improving crew safety. In addition, the watertight hull and the presence of a water evacuation pump allowed the FIAT 3000 to cross fords up to 1.1 metres deep, providing greater operational capability even in hostile environments.

Internally, the armoured space was divided into two parts by a firewall, isolating the combat compartment from the rear propulsion section. The driver's station, located at the front of the hull, offered the pilot an optimal view thanks to two side slits and a central hatch, which could be adjusted to improve visibility under travelling conditions. The tank commander, seated behind the pilot, had a height-adjustable seat and was able to start the engine from inside the vehicle, thus increasing operational flexibility. The engine compartment, located at the rear of the hull, housed the four-cylinder FIAT engine, characterised by a displacement of 6235 cm^3 and a power output of 45 horsepower at 1500 rpm and 50 horsepower at 1700 rpm for the Mod.21. Ignition was by a magnet, with different variants used depending on the model.

The FIAT 3000 was equipped with a complete transmission, including clutch, gearbox, differential and speed reducer. The clutch, an oil bath type with multiple discs, ensured efficient transmission of engine power to the wheels. The direct-drive gearbox offered three forward gears and a reverse gear, allowing the vehicle to adapt to different operating situations.

At the rear of the hull, a removable tail trench was installed, to which two removable lifting devices were attached. External equipment included a crank for starting the vehicle from the outside and a pickaxe, while the exhaust pipes were protected by shield plates to ensure greater strength and durability.

The FIAT 3000's **suspension** consisted of a system of metal spars riveted to the bottom of the hull, with an idler wheel at the front and a toothed wheel at the rear. Each spar rested on the load-bearing part of the track by means of eight rollers distributed in four bogies, assembled by means of terminal pins in the leaf springs of the suspension, stabilised by rubber buffers. This system allowed the vehicle to maintain a constant and uniform pressure on the rollers, ensuring a high degree of adaptability to different types of terrain.

Halfway up the hull was the second part of the tank, consisting of five load-bearing rollers supported by a small spar. This set was attached to the hull by means of a pin, which allowed the entire system to swivel. At the front of the set of idler rollers, the cross member was supported by a vertical spring, ensuring adequate track tension and giving it the elasticity needed to adapt to the terrain.

In the later models of the FIAT 3000, the track links were opened to provide better grip and greater ground pressure, thus improving the overall performance of the vehicle. The 360° turret contained the

▲ FIAT 3000 (left) and Renault FT, armed with SIA machine gun, for comparison. Fort Tiburtino (Rome), 1927.

FIAT LIGHT TANK (3000) (MODEL 1921), ITALY 1929

▲ FIAT 3000 in 1929 Mod. 21, an example with three-colour camouflage. The markings and number code - here painted on the hull sides - were white.

FIAT 3000 & FIAT 2000

armament, rear access hatch and attachments for the tank commander's seat. At the top, a dome provided openings for observation, ventilation and lighting, with the ability to open for improved internal ventilation or rapid evacuation in an emergency. The dome was perforated at the top centre to allow communication signals to pass through.

ARMAMENT

The FIAT 3000 Mod.21 initially employed two 6.5 mm SIA machine guns, each with an initial load of 2000 cartridges distributed in 50 40-round magazines (later increased to 91 40-round magazines). However, the difficulties encountered in loading the machine guns on the move and the unreliability of the weapons led to the search for a new armament. The FIAT Arsenal in Turin proposed the adoption of a pair of Lewis machine guns in 1922, but the project was not approved.

Subsequently, the Model 21 was adapted to accommodate two FIAT Mod.14/35 8mm calibre machine guns, fed by 80-round magazines (5760 rounds in total), with the gun tubes protected by armoured sleeves. This model had a distinctive configuration with the machine guns mounted higher on the turret and stronger suspension mounts. Regardless of the type of machine gun mounted, the armament was coupled in parallel on the same axis, with a collimator positioned between the two arms for coordinated firing.

However, during field manoeuvres in 1927, it became evident that the FIAT 3000 needed a heavier and more effective armament. Therefore, plans were made to equip the turret with a 37 mm Vickers-Terni cannon, which was considered state-of-the-art in Europe at the time. However, the additional weight of the cannon made the FIAT 3000 undersized and compromised cross-country performance, highlighting the need for engine improvements.

Consequently, in 1928, the FIAT Arsenal in Turin began planning substantial modifications, including a more powerful engine and a reworked turret. In 1930, the Italian military authorities ordered 52 tanks named FIAT 3000 Tank Model 1930, but due to the shortage of 37 mm cannons, only some of them were equipped with this armament, while others retained the machine guns of the previous model.

The FIAT 3000 Mod.30, equipped with the 37/40 cannon, had the main gun shifted to the right of the turret, with a gun elevation and depression of -10° to +20° and an armament of 68 37 mm rounds. However, difficulties with the armament and the overall performance of the vehicle led to its gradual replacement, with only a few remaining in service until 1935, when modifications were introduced during production and retrospectively.

In 1936, many early examples were equipped with the FIAT 14/35 machine gun, mounted higher on the turret and protected by armoured vests. However, both machine guns and 37 mm cannons soon proved unsatisfactory for use on Italian tanks, and by 1940 only two machine guns on tanks were considered inadequate, highlighting the need for further improvements in the armament and overall design of armoured vehicles.

FIAT 3000 A LIGHT TANK (MODEL 1921), SPAIN 1925

▲ The FIAT 300 was derived directly from the French FT-17, and was therefore conceived towards the end of the Great War. The tank had a fair amount of luck abroad. Among the countries involved was Spain: in 1925 this was the champion tank, renamed ATM 984, which was assigned to the 'Escuela central de Tiro' for various tests.

▲ FIAT four-cylinder in-line petrol engine, 6235 cm³. Web source.

▼ Longitudinal section of a FIAT 3000 Mod. 21. The two crew members can be seen. Web source.

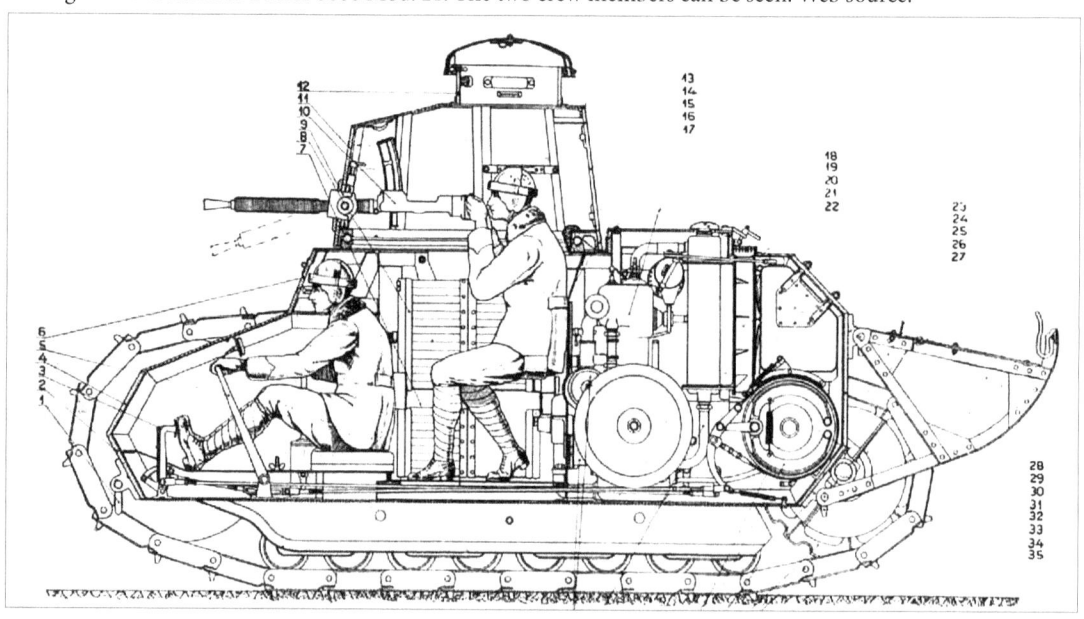

FIAT 3000 A LIGHT TANK (MODEL 1921), SPAIN 1925

▲ Il FIAT 300 derivava direttamente dal frenacese FT-17, concepito quindi verso la fine della Grande Guerra. Il carro ebbe una discreta fortuna all'esterio. GFra gi paesi interssati vi fu anche la Spagna, che nel 1925. Questo fu il carro campione, ribattezzato ATM 984 che venne assegnato alla "Escuela central de Tiro per i vari test.

FIAT 3000 LIGHT TANK (1930 MODEL), ITALY, ROME 1930

▲ FIAT 3000 mod. 1930 command tank of the 2nd Platoon 2nd Company of the 2nd Battalion Tank Regiment, Rome 1930. See photo page 14.

VERSIONS OF THE VEHICLE

The variants of the FIAT 3000 include a series of adaptations and modifications made to the basic vehicle to meet specific operational requirements or to experiment with new configurations. Although they represent only a few of the possible configurations of the FIAT 3000, they highlight the diversity of roles and functions the vehicle could assume based on the specific requirements of the operational environment and military strategies. Some of the most significant variants include:

1. **FIAT 3000 Mod. 21**: this was the initial version of the FIAT 3000, introduced in 1921. It was armed with two 6.5 mm SIA machine guns and later with two FIAT Model 14/35 8 mm machine guns. It had many limitations, including poor firepower and vulnerability.

2. **FIAT 3000 Mod. 30**: this version, introduced in 1930, featured several improvements over the Model 21. The main change was the adoption of a 37 mm Vickers-Terni cannon as the main weapon, instead of machine guns. This significantly improved the tank's firepower.

3. **FIAT 3000 Nebbiogeno (fog-maker)**: a smoke screen generation system was tested in 1925 during a major training exercise involving numerous Italian units. This system involved the use of two cylindrical tanks containing sulphuric acid, into which the exhaust gases produced by the engine were conveyed. The sulphuric acid and CO_2 generated by the engine reacted to create a thick curtain of white smoke. Later, on the occasion of the Chemical Army Day in Rome in 1935, some examples of the FIAT 3000 Model 1921 were modified with the addition of two smoke-curtain diffusers at the rear of the hull. However, neither variant was ever mass-produced.

▲ A FIAT 3000 model 30, armed with a 37 mm cannon, in command version, equipped with an impressive radio installation. The tank belongs to a Frontier Tank Company, deployed in the Balkans.

4. Lanciafiamme FIAT 3000 (flamethrower): version designed in 1932 by Major Rodolfo Foronato and Captain Enrico Riccardi of the Bologna Tank Regiment. This variant was equipped with a turret-mounted flamethrower. The vehicle retained its basic configuration, but was modified to house a tank of flammable liquid and a barrel for spraying fire at short range; this was positioned behind the engine compartment, in place of the iron tail. Protruding from the turret was a long barrel from which the flammable liquid was sprayed at high pressure. The flammable liquid tank had a capacity of 270 litres while the flamethrower had an average range of 6 hours and a range of 100 metres. This version was used to attack enemy trenches or protected targets.

5. FIAT 4000: designed in the late 1920s to transport medium-calibre artillery, but remained in the planning stage. The vehicle would have weighed 3 tonnes and used the same engine as the FIAT 3000.

▲ FIAT 3000 Model 1930 with radio antenna during training. FIAT 3000s equipped with this radio had an unusual antenna on the turret, which allowed it to rotate 360°. However, the communication range was limited to a few kilometres, which allowed communication between vehicles, but was not sufficient for collaboration with artillery and infantry, a key component of modern warfare.

FIAT 3000 LIGHT TANK (1930 MODEL) L5-30, ITALY, BOLOGNA 1933

▲ FIAT 3000 (1930 model) L5-30, 1st Tank Battalion, Command Tank 2nd Company - Bologna, Italy, 1933.

FIAT 3000 LIGHT TANK (1921 MODEL) IN TRIPOLITANIA, 1925

▲ FIAT 3000 (1921 model) armed with Lewis 2 x 77mm machine gun, assigned to the Tripolitania area in Libya, 1925.

▲ Front view of a FIAT 3000 Mod. 1921. Small photo: the FIAT 3000 described in the profile on the left.

FIAT 3000 LIGHT TANK, FOG VERSION, ITALY 1935

▲ FIAT 3000 in an early flamethrower version (note the tank in the lower area). This version was not mass-produced. Italy, 1935.

▲ Small photo: FIAT 3000 Model 21 tank in Montenegro. Note the white colouring of the turret cap, useful for aerial identification of the friendly vehicles (Benvenuti - Colonna). In the large photo: another image of FIAT 3000 of the Frontier Guard (probably the same tank as the previous photograph) in Montenegro.

FIAT 3000 LIGHT TANK (MODEL 1921) 1ST SERIES, ETHIOPIA 1935

▲ FIAT 3000 mod. 1921 1st series, Ethiopian Campaign 1935.

OPERATIONAL USE

The FIAT 3000 was mainly used in Italian colonies, such as East Africa and Libya, during the 1930s. However, by the start of the Second World War, it was already considered obsolete for the modern battlefield and was gradually replaced by more advanced armoured vehicles.

The FIAT 3000's baptism of fire took place in 1926, when two FIAT 3000s took part in operations to recapture the Giarabub Oasis in Libya. The Italian military expedition left on 1 February 1926, as a military column comprising 36 armoured vehicles (a squadron of Tripoli armoured cars, 8 armoured trucks, a section of 2 Ford T armoured cars) and 2 FIAT 3000s. The tanks slowed down the speed and advance of the entire column considerably, which did not give a good initial assessment.

After that, the FIAT 3000 was used in various operational contexts during its military career. Here is a summary of the main campaigns in which it was involved:

ETHIOPIAN WAR (1935-1936)

During this Italian-led colonial war against Ethiopia, the FIAT 3000 was one of the main tanks used by Italian forces. Although its armament could be considered limited by the standards of the time, the FIAT 3000 contributed to the support of infantry troops and the penetration of enemy territories. It is recalled that a small number of FIAT 3000s in 1936 met with other FIAT 3000s previously sold to the Ethiopian government, but no duel took place between them as the Ethiopian FIAT 3000s were unarmed.

SPANISH CIVIL WAR (1936-1939)

Italy provided military support to Spanish nationalists during the Civil War, and the FIAT 3000 was one of the tanks used by the Italian forces sent to Spain. However, its presence in these operations was not as significant as in other theatres of war.

▲ Real (uncoloured) photo of the FIAT 3000 with the 1935 modifications in the Balkans, 1941.

■ SECOND WORLD WAR (1939-1945)

At the beginning of the Second World War, the FIAT 3000 was already considered obsolete compared to new technological developments in the field of armoured vehicles. However, some examples were still used in the early stages of the conflict, mainly in second-line or internal security duties. Most FIAT 3000s were gradually withdrawn from active service during the course of the war, replaced by more modern models such as the M11/39 Tank.

■ ITALIAN OCCUPATION OF THE BALKANS (1941-1943)

After the invasion of Albania in 1939, Italy expanded its sphere of influence in the Balkans. During the occupation of the Balkan territories, the FIAT 3000 may have been used for patrol duties and riot control.

■ ALLIED INVASION OF SICILY (JULY 1943)

During the Allied invasion of Sicily in July 1943, Italian FIAT 3000 tanks were deployed against the Allied forces. Two companies, each with nine tanks, were deployed within the 6th Army. The 1st Company set up machine gun emplacements to defend the coast, while the 2nd Company defended an airfield. The tanks were involved in clashes with American paratroopers, but their slowness made them vulnerable. In the end, six tanks were lost and the other three were probably abandoned or destroyed. The Italians, with antiquated tanks, could not effectively counter the Allied invasion, which included modern tanks such as the Sherman.

▲ A rare picture of a FIAT 3000 tank of the CCCXII Mixed Tank Battalion manoeuvring in Rhodes (Pedonesi family archive).

▲ A command tank, recognisable by its conspicuous antenna on the French Front in June 1940 (ACS).

▼ Line of FIAT 3000s armed with cannon. Italy in the 1930s.

▲▼ Two FIAT 3000 belonging to the Ronchetti column assigned to the oasis of Giarabub, Libya, 1926. Below: Also in Giarabub, Libya, some FIAT 3000 Model 1921s participating in the conquest of Giarabub in 1926. The first vehicle on the left is armed with a Lewis machine gun. Source italie1935. Author's colouring.

In general, although the FIAT 3000 played an important role in the early stages of Italian armoured force development, its operational utility diminished over the years, mainly due to technological advances in the field of armoured vehicles. However, during its early stages of deployment, the FIAT 3000 contributed significantly to Italian military strategy, providing an important experience base for the development of future Italian tanks.

▲ A Frontier Guard tank officer poses in front of a FIAT 3000 tank in Montenegro in the winter of 1941 - 1942.

▲ Two FIAT 3000s deployed in Makallè, Ethiopia, 1937 after the conquest of the Negus empire.

▼ Beautiful picture of two FIAT 3000s in exercise with Italian infantry in the late 1930s. Author's colouring.

▲ A FIAT 3000 under repair in the Ethiopian theatre of war 1935.

▲ The small size of the vehicle, which forced the crew to perform complicated manoeuvres to enter the vehicle, is very well appreciated in this picture.

▲ FIAT 3000 profile seen from above, cannon version.

FIAT 3000 & FIAT 2000

FIAT 3000 LIGHT TANK (1930 MODEL) ITALY, SICILY 1943

▲ FIAT 3000 mod. L5-30 belonging to XII Battalion L tanks, mobile group A, Sicily, July 1943.

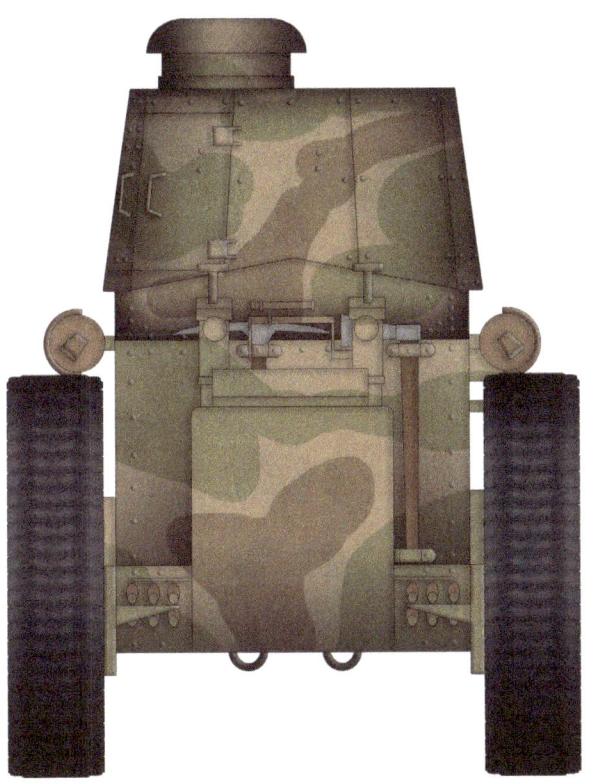

▲ Front and rear profile view of the FIAT 3000.

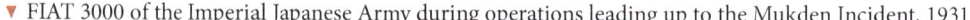
▲ FIAT 3000 Model 1921 of the 2nd Company just captured by the US army at the airport of Licata, Sicily in 1943. Source italie1935-45.

▼ FIAT 3000 of the Imperial Japanese Army during operations leading up to the Mukden Incident, 1931.

▲ Near the church of St Maurice in Montgenévre, Italian soldiers pose next to a FIAT 3000 model 21 of the 4th Frontier Carrista Company, after the occupation of Montgenévre in June 1940.

FIAT 3000 LIGHT TANK (MODEL 1921), ALBANIA 1941

▲ FIAT 3000 (model 1921) assigned to the Frontier Guard 1st Platoon, 1st Company in Albania in 1941.

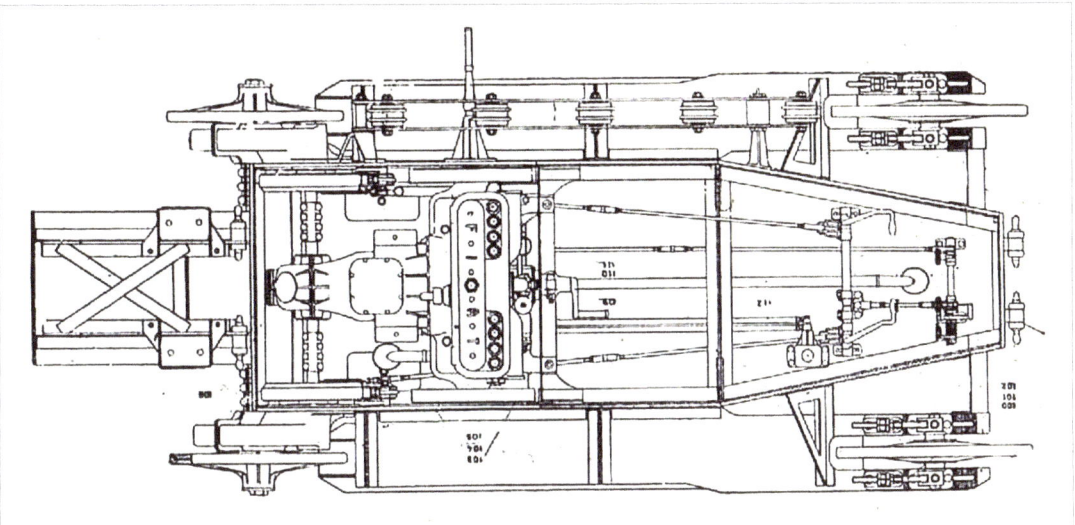

▲ Sectional view of the FIAT 3000 from the original service and operating manual.

▼ Another obsolete FIAT 3000 model 21 (probably from the 1st Frontier Carrista Company of the G.A.F.) on the impassable Balkan terrain in 1941 (Benvenuti - Colonna). Author's colouring.

FIAT 3000 & FIAT 2000

FIAT 3000 LIGHT TANK (MODEL 1921), HUNGARY 1931

▲ Hungarian FIAT 3000. The first FIAT 3000 light tanks that arrived in Hungary were delivered with the national livery and colouring and without any weapons.

▲ The crew of a FIAT 3000 poses for a souvenir photo in 1930 in Italy. Note the insignia already of the perimeter-only type, and no longer in full colour.

▶ A FIAT 3000 loaded on its special transport trolley pulled by a military truck. Author's colouring.

▲ A FIAT 3000 that tipped over, remaining as if nailed in the ground during testing. Author's colouring.

FIAT 3000 LIGHT TANK (MODEL 1921), HUNGARY 1931

▲ Hungarian FIAT 3000s were equipped with the Hungarian camouflage tricolour and/or green background colour. The Hungarians mounted as their default weapon the Maschinengewehr Patent Schwarzlose M.07/12, which they knew well, as it was the service weapon of the Austro-Hungarian monarchy.

FIAT 3000 & FIAT 2000

FIAT 3000 LIGHT TANK (1921 MODEL SERIES 2), ITALY, SICILY 1943

▲ FIAT 3000 mod. L5-21 2nd Series, armed with two S.I.A. 6.5mm MG machine guns - Sicily, summer 1943.

CAMOUFLAGE AND DISTINGUISH MARKS

Because the FIAT 3000 was used in so many units and for so many years, the various colour combinations used to finish the vehicles were numerous. One of the earliest camouflage schemes for the Model 21 tanks was rather unusual, with numerous irregular patches of green (FS 14036) and brown (FS 30176) - some with borders in other colours - almost entirely covering the yellow ochre base (FS33696). However, this scheme was soon replaced by two-coloured 'wave' camouflage, applied at the factory in various patterns, sometimes with vertical stripes on the hull and horizontal stripes for the turret. It was a rather simple disruptive design with a high tonal contrast.

The 'wave' pattern did not last long and was replaced by the more traditional red-brown coat (FS 30109) in the mid-1930s. This colour, a dark brick red brown, tended to take on an almost chocolate brown hue when freshly applied and could fade to a pinkish hue over time. The photos provided sufficient evidence that new camouflage patterns were adopted for a number of years from 1935 onwards. The red-brown base colour could be speckled or flecked with dark green (FS 14036), and the pattern seemed to vary quite a bit, following the personal taste of individual painters, with more or less blurred spots or splashes of green. A rare camouflage, associated with a late Model 30 tank series, had numerous small green (FS 14036) and brown (FS 30152) spots on the red-brown background.

After 1937, tanks began to be painted with the new dark grey-green (FS 34062) common to most armoured equipment of the time. This colour, a medium green with a pronounced grey hue, had a semi-gloss finish when freshly painted, but could soon deteriorate to a dull, faded finish. In June 1940, FIAT 3000 tanks in service were painted grey-green or red-brown; some tanks appeared to have a very faded splash of grey-green on red-brown or retained their old red-brown and dark green camouflage. The Frontier Guard retained the camouflage and markings of the other armoured units, so their tanks were grey-green with few differences.

■ MEDIUM AND LIGHT TANK BADGES

The new Army units emphasised the importance of tactical marking, so the Regio Esercito extended the practice to FIAT 3000 tanks between 1925 and 1926. Tactical symbols - a series of complete colour-coded geometric figures - painted in four positions on Models 21 and 30, and only in three on Model 30 were introduced. The two squadrons (later companies) in a battalion were marked in red for the 1st and in white for the 2nd. The company commander's tanks had a circle, while those of the platoon commander

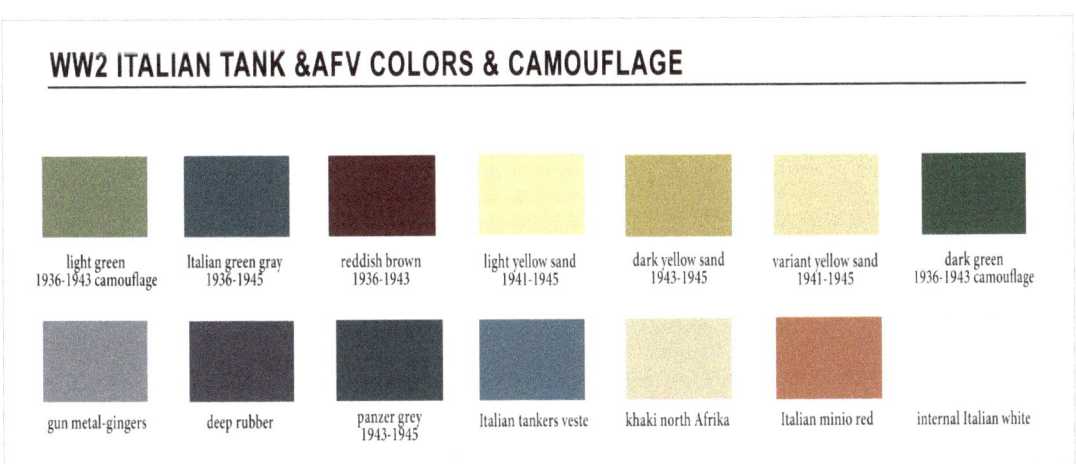

had a triangle, pointing upwards for the 1st company and downwards for the 2nd. Within the platoon, the tanks were marked by a series of stripes - from one to three -, horizontal for the 1st and vertical for the 2nd. The tactical signals were accompanied by a code number, painted in the company colour on the bottom of the side frames or, rarely, on the hull side plates and on the bow. The first was a Roman numeral (for battalion) followed by two Arabic numerals, for platoon and individual tanks, there were two separating dots between the numbers. The style could be slightly different from the prescribed one, e.g. without dots. Any tank could be quickly identified, but this method was of great help to enemy intelligence services, so in the mid-1930s the code numbers were usually omitted. Shortly before the start of the Italian attack on Ethiopia, the new 'hollow' markings were adopted, which mimicked the earlier ones but with only the outline, to make them less visible; however, the sharp edges were still sometimes too visible. However, some older tanks still bore these marks until 1939, although they were not very often seen at that time. To complicate matters further, from 1937 the standard camouflage colour for tanks became grey-green and the markings changed again to the typical 'rectangular' system that remained in use for all Italian tanks until the armistice of September 1943.

All Italian AFVs had a stamped metal plate; the tank of the FIAT 3000 was initially rectangular, 58 x 13 cm, riveted and fixed by brackets on the right side of the hull. The background was enamelled white, with the inscription 'Ro To' in red (the initials stood for Regio Esercito) followed by black numbers and a red printed A. All lines were 10 cm high and the numbers ranged from 1 to 51 and 53 to 109 for the Model 21 tanks and 108 to 154 for the Model 30. There is no official list, but examples of Model 30 tanks with numbers ranging from 126 to 149 are documented. The second and last type of plate was adopted from 1934 in the form of a square measuring approximately 23 x 15 cm, also riveted to the right side of the hull, just below the turret. Small variations included a new red flaming grenade, while the letter A was omitted; the numbers remained in the bottom line. Model 21 serial numbers ranged from 1001 to 1120, while Model 30 serial numbers ranged from 1111 to 1154, with tank numbers from 1128 to 1151. Some exceptions include at least two tanks numbered 2599 and 2750.

Depending on the period, three metal badges were presented on the FIAT 3000's tanks, arranged in different configurations. First, the logo of FIAT (the tank manufacturer), applied to a small oval metal plate; over the years, it was sometimes repainted in the basic tank colour and sometimes served as a back plate for a welded Tank Corps badge. Another badge was common to all military vehicles of the Royal Army: after a brief appearance of a paper badge, a metal badge was adopted from March 1936. This circular relief plate, cast in bronze with a diameter of 12.4 cm, was riveted onto a back plate. The badge depicted the fascio littorio, a five-pointed star and the initials 'Ro To'. A third, non-regulation badge consisted of the corps' own coat of arms, a graceful bronze casting measuring 12.5 x 17 cm, welded to the tank turret in various positions during the FIAT 3000's long service.

▲ Symbols used from 1925 to 1928 on the FIAT 3000. From 1928 to 1938 the figures were only outlined along the ptofile and no longer filled in with colour. Source: zimmerit.com

▲ The Hungarian FIAT 3000 light tanks received a two-digit number plate starting with H-. In the early 1940s, the light tanks were used for basic driving and mechanical training, at which point the turrets were removed. Small photo: Two FIAT 3000 tanks belonging to the Hungarian army, with typical Hungarian three-colour camouflage and national insignia. They still lack the weapon as the Hungarians mounted Schwarzloses. (Bonhardt)

FIAT 3000 LIGHT TANK (LF) L5 FLAMETHROWER VERSION, ITALY 1935

▲ A FIAT 3000 tank of the 1st Frontier Tank Company in Durres, Albania, in 1940 (Crippa).

▼ During the Second World War, the Regio Esercito still employed some aliquots of the old FIAT 3000 tanks. In the photograph one of these tanks, in charge of a Frontier Guard unit in the Balkans in 1941.

FIAT 3000 LIGHT TANK (MODEL II), ITALY 1940

▲ FIAT 3000 mod. L5-30 belonging to XII Battalion L tanks, mobile group A, Sicily, July 1943.

PRODUCTION AND EXPORT

Despite improvements over the Renault FT, from which it was derived, the FIAT 3000 did not achieve the same success on the international market as the French model. This was largely due to the rapid absoloescence of the vehicle, which was soon outdated in concept and technology. In addition, its production remained more limited than the Renault FT, which was available in larger quantities. Around twenty FIAT 3000s were sold or transferred abroad, but none of them were able to meet the needs of the respective armies for which they were intended.

Italy: as always, the main user was the country of origin of the vehicle. After the first test run in 1920, the tank entered service in 1921. At the time of the order, 1,200 were ordered in 1918, but the end of World War I reduced the order to 150. The first tanks were delivered to the army in 1922 and the first actual deployment took place in 1926 in Libya as part of anti-war operations.

Albania: two Model 1921s were sold to Albania in the late 1920s together with some old Bianchi armoured cars, and were later recovered during the Italian occupation of Albania in 1939.

Argentina: a FIAT 3000 Model 1921 was delivered to Argentina, equipped with a FIAT Model 1924 machine gun. The tank paraded in Buenos Aires during Argentina's national holiday on 25 May 1924.

Denmark: in 1928, some Danish military technicians, having seen it at work two years earlier in Turin, purchased a FIAT 3000 Mod. 21 armed with two 6.5 mm SIA machine guns at a cost of 30,500 Danish crowns. However, this model was already excluded from military exercises in 1929. It was then slightly modified, but by 1932 it was no longer even on the staff, probably used for machine-gun training.

Ethiopia: in 1925, the Ethiopian Empire purchased a Mod. 21, to which three more FIAT 3000 Mod. 30s were added in 1930, both models armed with machine guns (the model included the installation of these weapons, but they were probably all supplied without armament), all of which were later recovered in 1936 with the invasion of Ethiopia.

Greece: there is not much information available on the Greek FIAT 3000.

Hungary: in 1931, Hungary purchased five FIAT 3000s, which formed a Tank Company together with German LK II tanks. The five examples were supplied without armament. The remains of one example used as a target are preserved today at the artillery range in Várpalota.

Lithuania: In 1926, six Mod. 21s were ordered and delivered in September 1927. Their operational history is unknown, but they were probably later turned over to Hungary under Italian arrangements.

Japan: the Japanese purchased a FIAT 3000 for testing, which then participated in the Sino-Japanese War.

Spain: the Spanish army purchased a FIAT 3000 for testing, ordered in October 1924. Delivered in 1925, it was registered as ATM 984 and destined for the Escuela Central de Tir. It was then used until the Spanish Civil War.

URSS: in 1927, the USSR purchased three FIATs, which were later equipped with 37 mm Hotchkiss guns. Another Model 1921 was donated to the USSR by the Polish Communist Party and participated in the parade on Moscow's Red Square in 1928. Two tanks were sent to the course academy for armoured commanders in 1929.

▲ A FIAT 3000 light tank in service in Hungary in the mid-1930s; the soldier wears the Italian model leather helmet, a distinctive piece of the uniform of armoured/armoured troops. (Author's collection)

▼ Summer 1939, Hungarian troops parade in Kassa (Kosice), FIAT 3000 light tanks are transported on two-wheeled trailers, pulled by a heavy truck. (Author's collection)

DATA SHEET FIAT 3000	
	FIAT 3000 Mod.1921 (Mod. 1930)
Dimensions	4,17 (4,29) x 1,64 (1,70) x 2,19 (2,20) m
Weight	5.5 (5.9) tonnes
Crew	2 (captain and pilot)
Engine	FIAT 304 petrol 50 hp (63 hp)
Maximum road speed	21 (22) kilometres per hour
Autonomy	95 (88) kilometres
Armament	2 x 6.5 mm SIA Model 1918 or 2 x 8 mm FIAT-Revelli Model 1914/1935 (1x 37/40 Vickers-Terni gun Model 1918)
Armour	Hull: 16 mm front, sides and rear. Roof and tail 8 mm. Floor: 6 mm. Turret: 16 mm front and sides. Roof 8 mm.
Production	100 Model 1921 and 52 Model 1930

DATA SHEET FIAT 2000	
Dimensions	7.4 m x 3.1 m x 3.8 m
Weight	38 tonnes
Crew	8
Engine	FIAT A12 petrol engine, six cylinders, 21 200 cm^3
Maximum road speed	7.5 kilometres per hour
Autonomy	75 km
Armament	Primary: 1 × 65/17 cannon Secondary: 7 × FIAT-Revelli Mod. 1914 machine guns
Armour	min 15 mm - max 20 mm
Production	2

▲ A FIAT 3000 towed by a FIAT 18 BLR truck belonging to a column of black shirts.

BIBLIOGRAPHY

- Nicola Pignato, *Storia dei mezzi corazzati,* Fratelli Fabbri editori, 1976, pp. 81-88.
- Antonio e Andrea Tallillo, D.Guglielmi, Flavio Chistè *Carro FIAT 3000. Sviluppo, tecnica, impiego.* GMT Trento 2018.
- Lorenzo Bovi, Antonio e Andrea Tallillo, Enrico Finazzer Cavalleria, *FIAT 3000 e altri mezzi. SICILIA. WW2. Seconda guerra mondiale.* Editore Ardite 2022.
- Maurizio Parri, Filippo Cappellano *IL PRIMO SECOLO DEL RIPARTO CARRI ARMATI.* Editore indipendente 2023.
- Bruno Benvenuti e Ugo F. Colonna - *L'armamento italiano nella seconda guerra mondiale Carri armati in servizio fra le due guerre 1* - Edizioni Bizzarri, Roma 1972
- Maurizio Parri, *Tracce di cingolo - compendio di generale di storia dei carristi 1919-2009*, Assocarri, 2009
- Filippo Cappellano, *Gli autoveicoli da combattimento dell'Esercito Italiano, vol.1*, Ufficio Storico dello Stato Maggiore dell'Esercito, Roma 2002.
- S.M.R.E. - *"Nozioni di armi, tiro e materiali vari",* Edizioni Le "Forze Armate", Roma, 1942.
- I. Di Nisio - *"I carri armati nel combattimento"*, in Manualetti di tecnica e cultura militare, fascicolo XVI, Ed. Rivista Esercito e Nazione, Istituto Poligrafico dello Stato, Roma, 1931.
- N. Pignato, *"I mezzi blindo-corazzati italiani 1923-1943"*, Albertelli Edizioni Speciali, Parma, 2004.
- Ralph E Jones, George H Rarey, Robert J. Icks: *The fighting Tanks since 1916.*
- John Joseph Timothy Sweet, Iron Arm: *The Mechanization of Mussolini's Army, 1920-1940*, Stackpole Books, 2007
- Filippo Cappellano, Pier Paolo Battistelli, *Italian Light Tanks: 1919-45,* Osprey Publishing, 2012.
- Emiliano Ciaralli Le Forze Armate, 1935 – Colonel Pederzini, Italian Tanks 1917-1945.
- Ministero della Guerra, Manuale Tecnico *CARRO ARMATO FIAT 3000 Mod 21 e 30 1931* Roma 1931
- AA.VV. *Il carro armato FIAT-2000. Dal 1917 alla costruzione della replica. Tank master special (Vol. 10).* Archivio Sroia 2022.
- Nico Sgarlato *Corazzati Italiani 1939-1945*, War Set n°10, 2006.
- David Vannucci, *Corazzati e blindati italiani dalle origini allo scoppio della seconda guerra mondiale*, Editrice Innocenti, 2003.
- Daniele Guglielmi & David Zambon, *Les véhicules blindés italiens 1910/43 (1ère partie)*, Batailles & Blindés n°24, 2008.
- Lucio Ceva & Andrea Curami, *La meccanizzazione dell'esercito dalle origini al 1943, Tomo II*, USSME, 1994
- Ugo Barlozzetti & Alberto Pirella *Mezzi dell'Esercito Italiano 1935-45*, Editoriale Olimpia, 1986
- Ralph Riccio, Marcello Calzolari e Nicola Pignato, *talian Tanks and Combat Vehicles of World War II*, Roadrunner Mattioli, 2010
- Gabriele De Rosa, *Storia dell'Ansaldo 6. Dall'IRI alla guerra, 1930-1945*, Editori Laterza, 1999
- Paolo Crippa e Carlo Cucut *I reparti corazzati italiani nei Balcani,* Soldiershop 2019.
- Paolo Crippa. *I reparti corazzati del R.E. E l'armistizio 1° Volume,* Soldiershop 2021.
- Paolo Crippa. *I reparti corazzati del R.E. E l'armistizio 2° Volume,* Soldiershop 2021.

ALREADY PUBLISHED TITLES

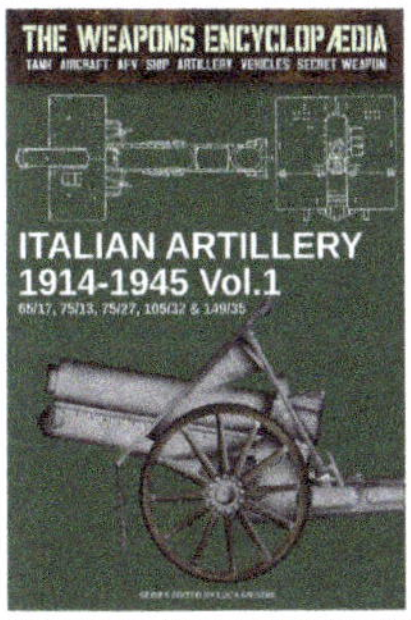

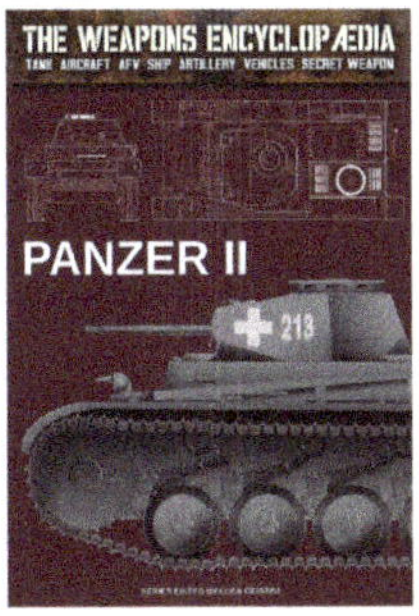

- ITALIAN LIGHT TANKS CV L3/33-35-38
- FOCKE-WULF FW 190
- SEMOVENTE 75/18 & 75/34
- ITALIAN MEDIUM TANK M13-40, M14-41 & M15-42
- PANZER III
- ITALIAN ARTILLERY 1914-1945 Vol.1
- PANZER II
- SOMUA S35
- FIAT C.R. 42 "FALCO"
- ITALIAN LIGHT TANK L6-40 & SEMOVENTE L40
- THE FIRST ITALIAN ARMOURED CARS: LANCIA 1Z, FIAT 611 AND OTHERS
- ITALIAN MEDIUM TANK M11-39
- HUNGARIAN TANKS TOLDI & TURAN
- PANZER 38 (t)
- ITALIAN ARTILLERY 1914-1945 Vol.2
- MATILDA MK II BRITISH TANK
- RUSSIAN LIGHT TANK T-26
- MESSERSCHMITT BF 109 Vol. 1 SERIE A-B-C-D-E
- M3 LEE/GRANT US MEDIUM TANK
- SEMOVENTI ITALIANI 2
- STUG III SD.KFZ. 142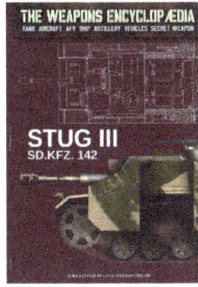
- BLINDATI UNGHERESI ZRINYI E CSABA
- FIAT 3000 E FIAT 2000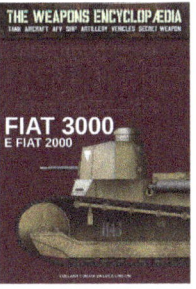
- CANNONI ITALIANI 1914-1945 Vol.3

TWE-023 EN

www.ingramcontent.com/pod-product-compliance
Ingram Content Group UK Ltd.
Pitfield, Milton Keynes, MK11 3LW, UK
UKHW060216240426
12048UKWH00030BB/1690